Clip Art Assembly Basics

Here are some suggestions to help you as you make your flyers, annc
clip art from this book.

Tools

Putting together the right tools for the project will make it go smoother and look better in the end. A good **copy machine** is a must. It's worth the extra effort to make sure your school or copy shop has machines that make clean copies. You will also need a bottle of white **paper correction fluid**, a fine-tip **black marker** to combine the designs and add your own art to the project, **rubber cement** to mount the design onto your paper during the layout stage of your project, and **scissors** for cutting apart the designs you choose. Optional tools to help create a professional-looking job are a **non-reproducible blue pencil** to make marks that will not show up on copies that you make, a **proportion scale** to help you determine the size of the reduction or enlargement necessary to fit your paper, and a **blue grid pad** for laying out the project with straight lines.

Assembly Steps

1. Choose the design or designs you will be putting together for the project that you will be making.

2. Copy the design as it is from the book so that you have one copy from which to work without having to cut apart your book.

3. Cut out the designs you have selected for your project and lay them out on your paper. (This is where the blue grid paper comes in handy.) A light table can also help with the layout of your page. If there is one available, take advantage of it.

4. At this point, make a copy of the designs and any text you have put on the paper before adding any other hand-drawn illustrations. Trying to draw over the grid paper lines is difficult and generally doesn't turn out well.

5. Now you have a pretty good idea of what your project is going to look like. Go ahead and add all the extra finishing touches. Small doodles drawn on each page of **Clip Art for Spring and Summer** will give you some ideas of what you can add to your paper. Even the most simple little dots or squares can really "warm up" the page and keep it from looking choppy.

6. Make your final copies of the page. Easy!

Hints

Keep a ¼ inch margin on all edges of your paper.

If the edges of the cut-out pieces are visible on your copies, lighten the copy machine one notch or use correction fluid on one copy and then use it to make final copies.

Removable tape is great for doing layout if you will be using the design over and over again.

Have fun with your projects! Even if you are not an artist, this is a great way to create something without having to have a huge amount of artistic ability.

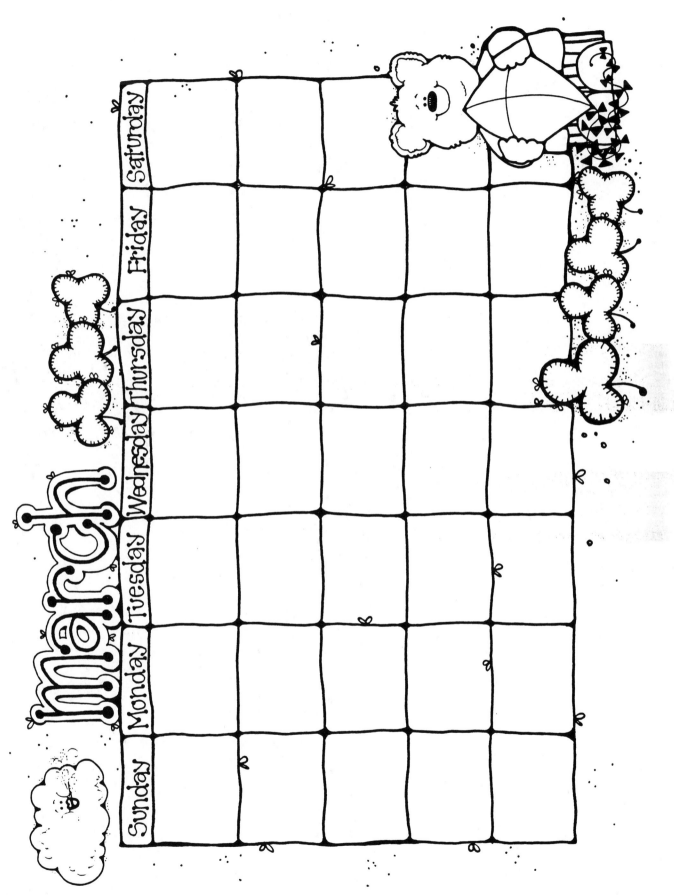

March

Sunday	Monday	Tuesday	Wednesday	Thursday	Friday	Saturday

3

March Birthdays

`Calendar cut·outs`

7

LOTS O' LUCK

11

13

A Message to Parents

21

HAPPY St. PATRICK'S DAY!

23

LUCK O' THE IRISH

25

27

HAPPY St. PATRICK'S DAY !

fold

35

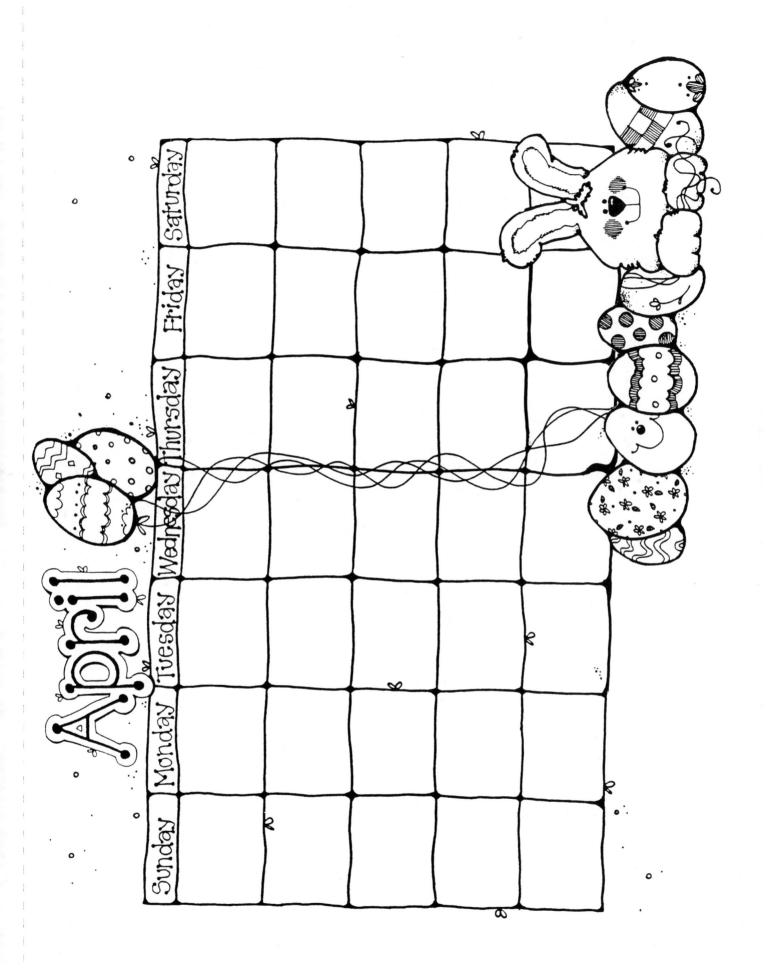

April

Sunday	Monday	Tuesday	Wednesday	Thursday	Friday	Saturday

April Birthdays

39

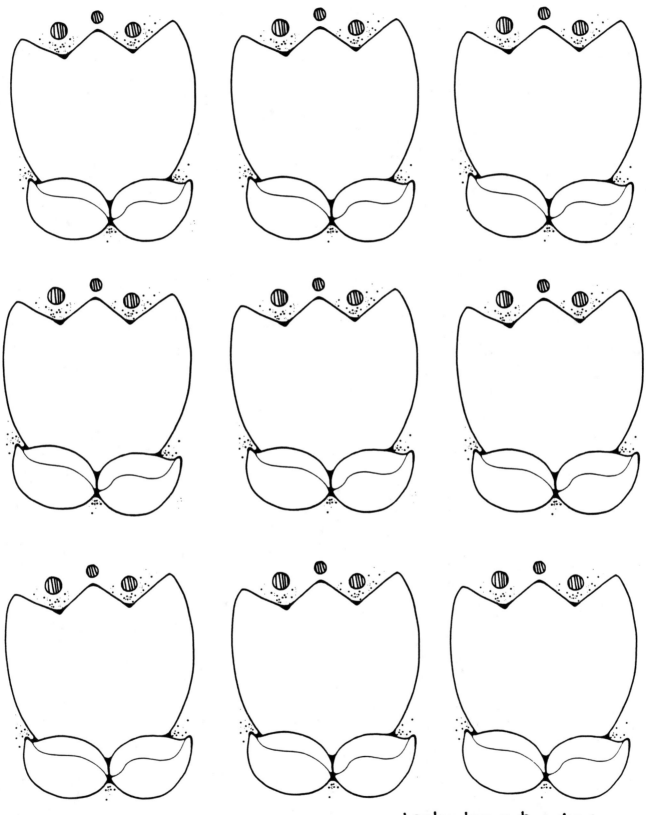

'calendar cut-outs'

41

43

fold

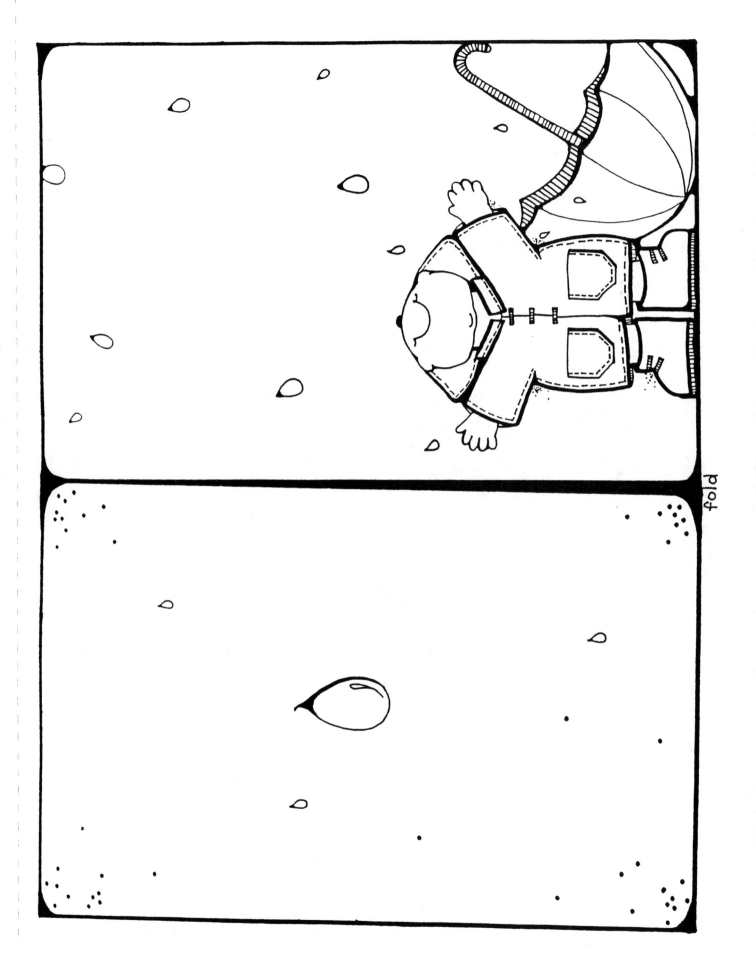

fold

SPRING SHOWERS

49

Happy Easter

from your teacher

fold

51

HAPPY EASTER

HAPPY EASTER

53

So Me buhhy special!

55

57

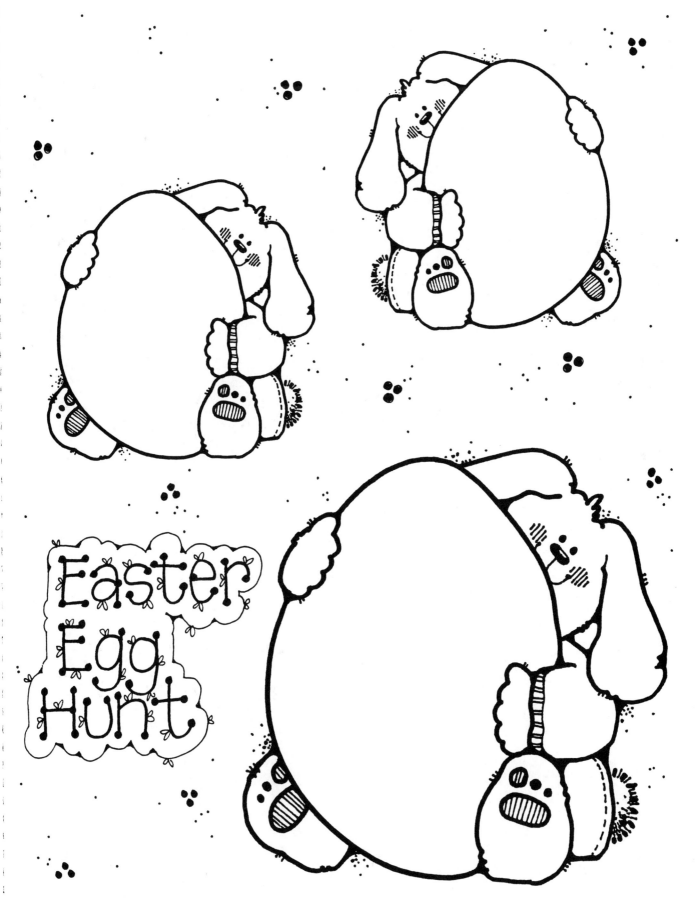

Easter Egg Hunt

"Some BUNNY Special"!

63

Especially for you!

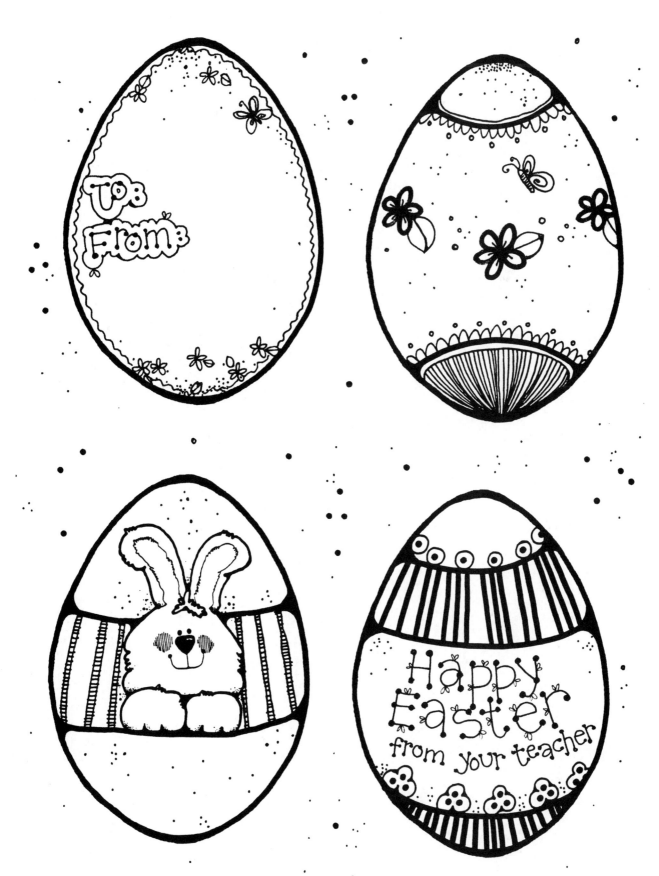

To
From

Happy
Easter
from your teacher

69

Happy Easter!

73

75

79

83

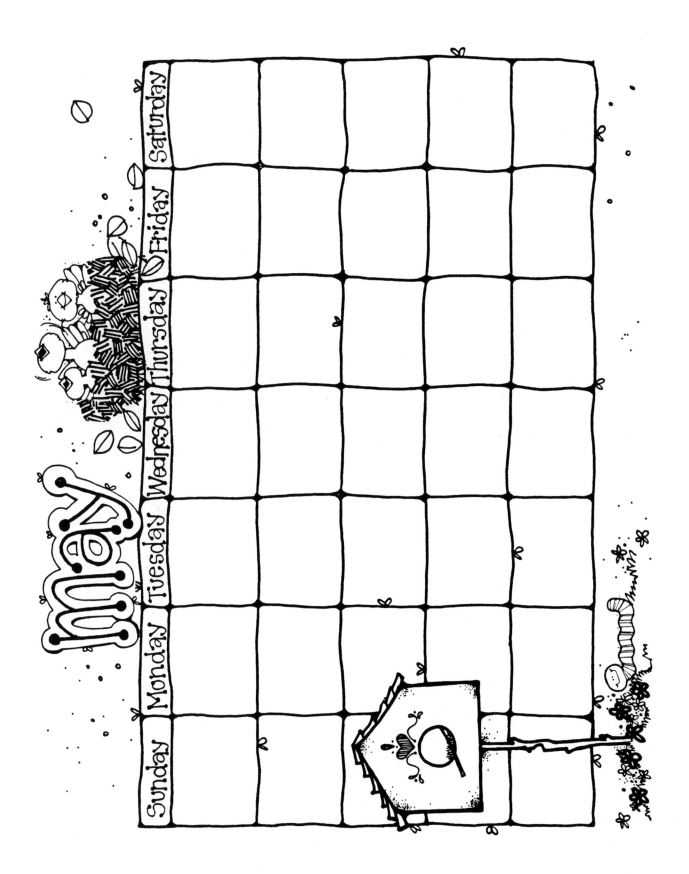

May

Sunday	Monday	Tuesday	Wednesday	Thursday	Friday	Saturday

May Birthdays

91

Happy Mother's Day

93

I love my mom because.....

97

I ♥ MY MOM

I ♥ MY MOM

Happy Mother's Day!

Happy Mother's Day!

#1 MOM

#1 MOM

101

Just for you!

105

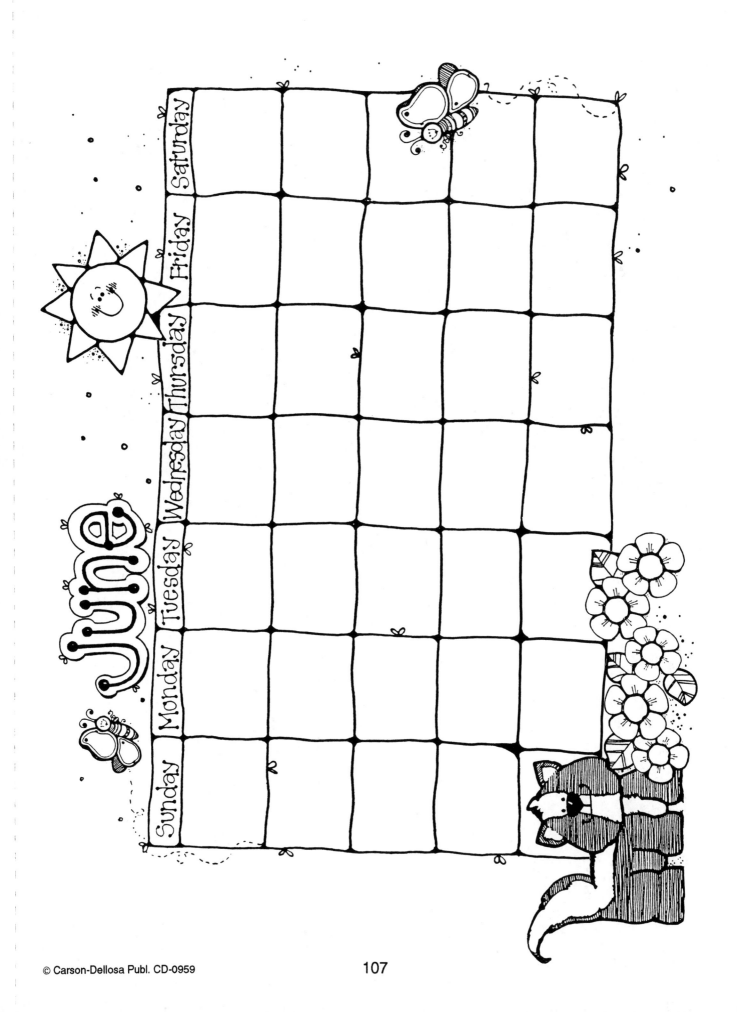

June

Sunday | Monday | Tuesday | Wednesday | Thursday | Friday | Saturday

June Birthdays

109

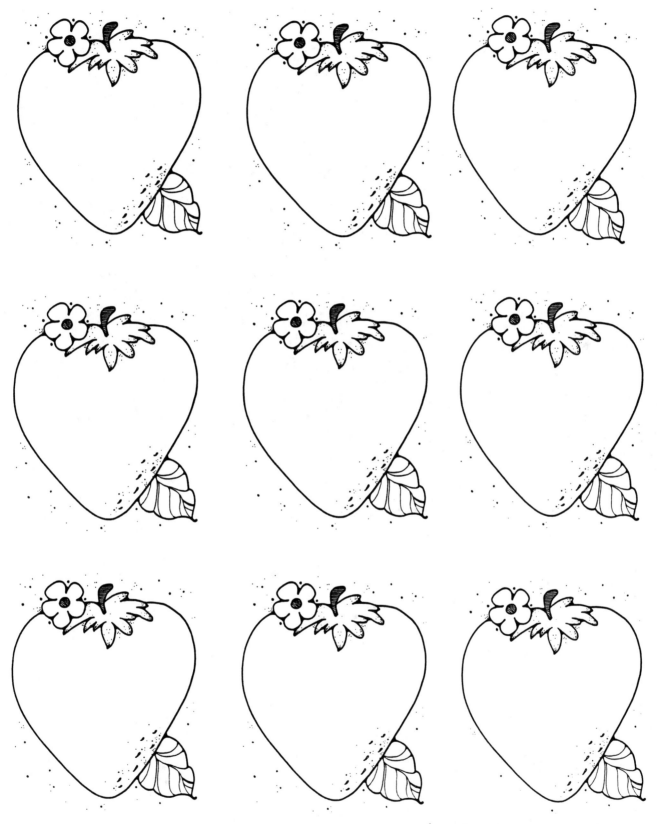

'calendar cut-outs'

115

THANK·YOU!
"Berry Much!"

fold

117

119

121

Father's Day

Father's Day

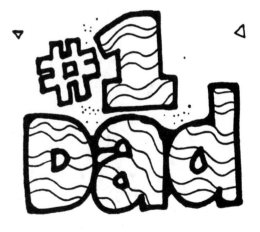

I love my Dad because......

125

Happy Father's Day

This coupon good for...

_____

With love from...

_____

Happy Father's Day

This coupon good for...

_____

With love from...

_____

Happy Father's Day

This coupon good for...

_____

With love from...

_____

133

fold

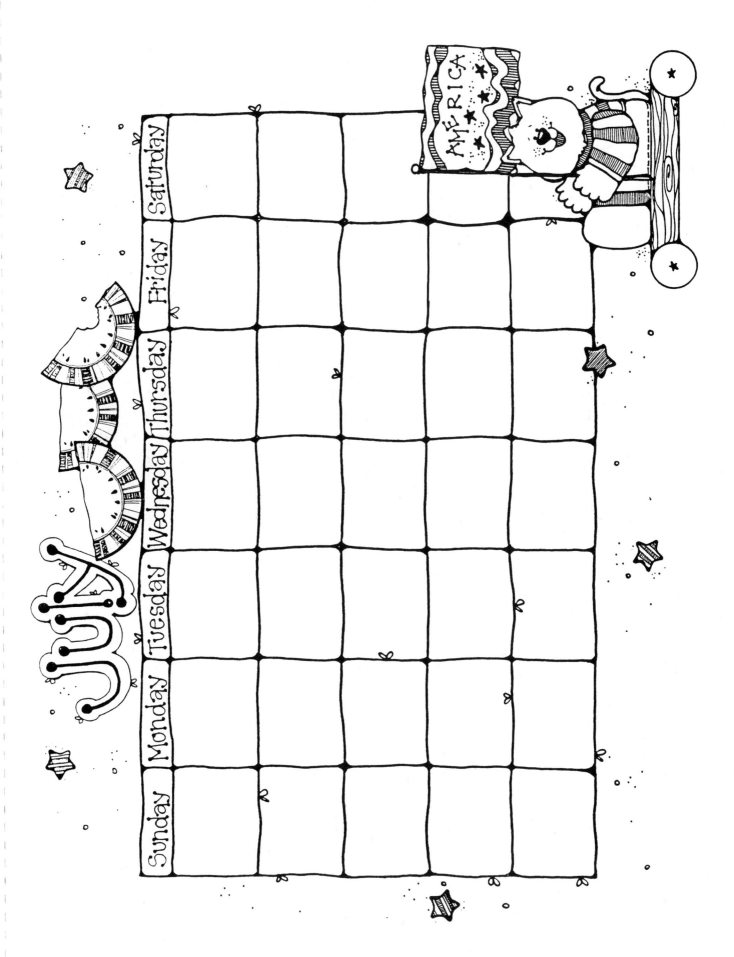

135

July Birthdays

137

HAPPY BIRTHDAY AMERICA !

143

LABOR DAY

147

Beach Party!

149

151

153

155

157

HELP !

We need the following for our class...

163

165

169

Thanks for your help!

fold

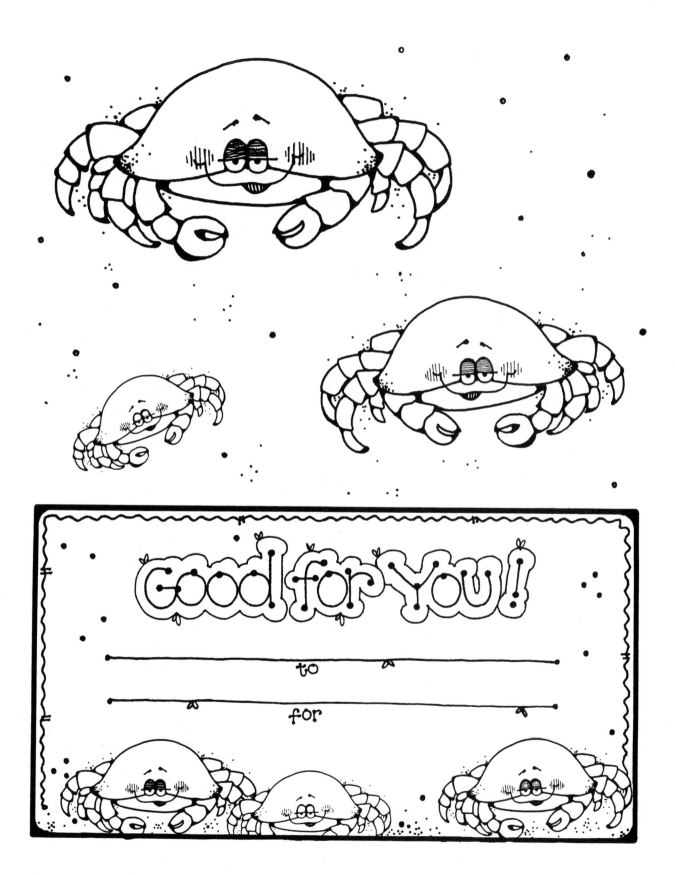

Good for you!

to _____

for _____

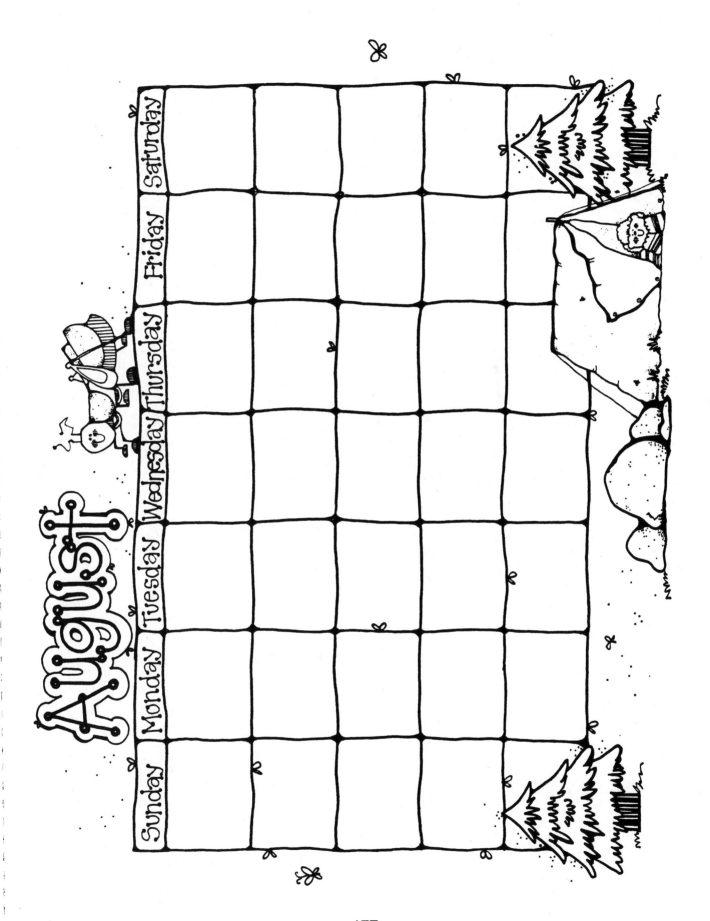

August

Sunday	Monday	Tuesday	Wednesday	Thursday	Friday	Saturday

August Birthdays

181

DAY CAMP NEWS

185

187

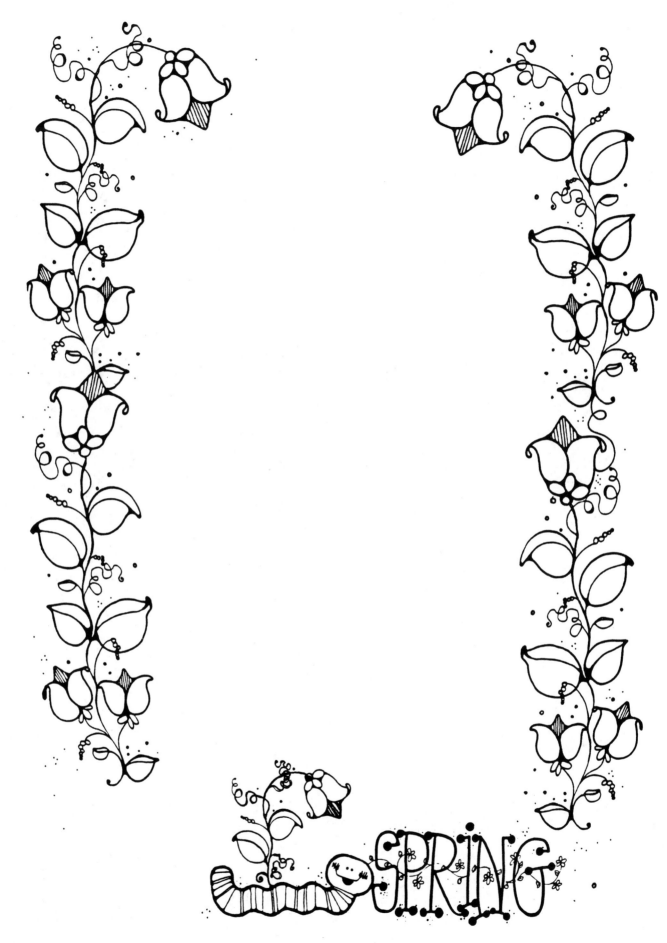

SPRING

201

SPRINGTIME NEWS

203

You're Invited

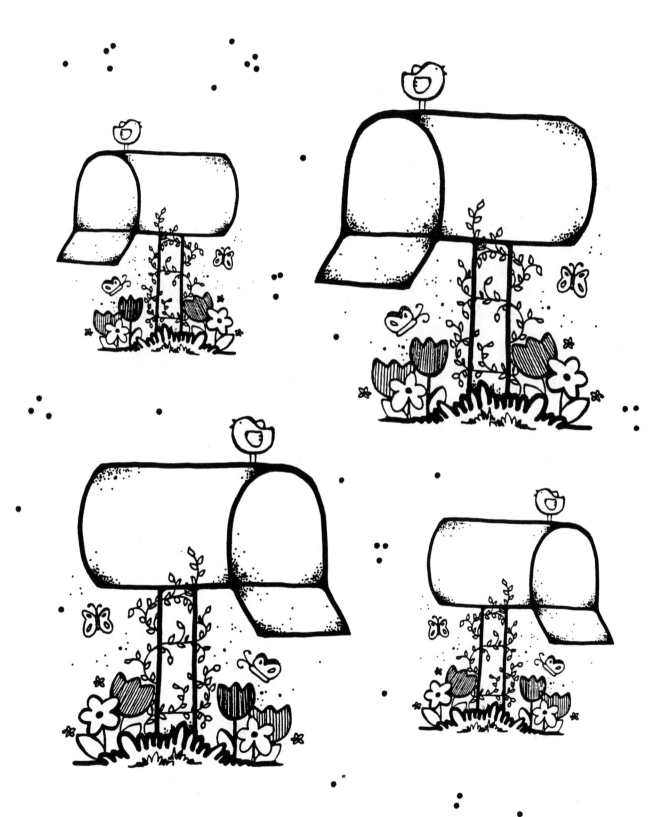

213

announcing...

A note to Parents...

Field Trip
Permission Form

Destination: _____

Date: _____

Special Instructions: _____

_____

_____

_____

Student: _____

Parent's Signature:

_____

News to the Parents

221

a note from... your teacher

fold

233

A Note to Parents

I know my address

_____
name

_____
street

_____
city & state

_____
zip

241

It's Especially for YOU!

fold

Home sweet Home

245

247

Thanks for your help!

JUST FOR YOU

253

257

SUMMER NEWS

259

MY SUMMER VACATION

BY

DATE

SUMMER SCHOOL

265

How I spent my summer....

269

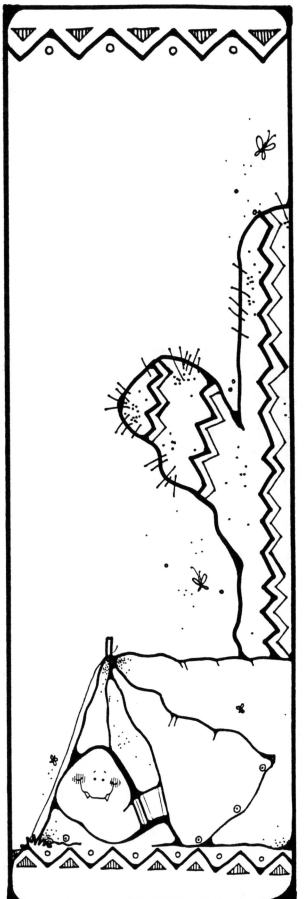

fold

281

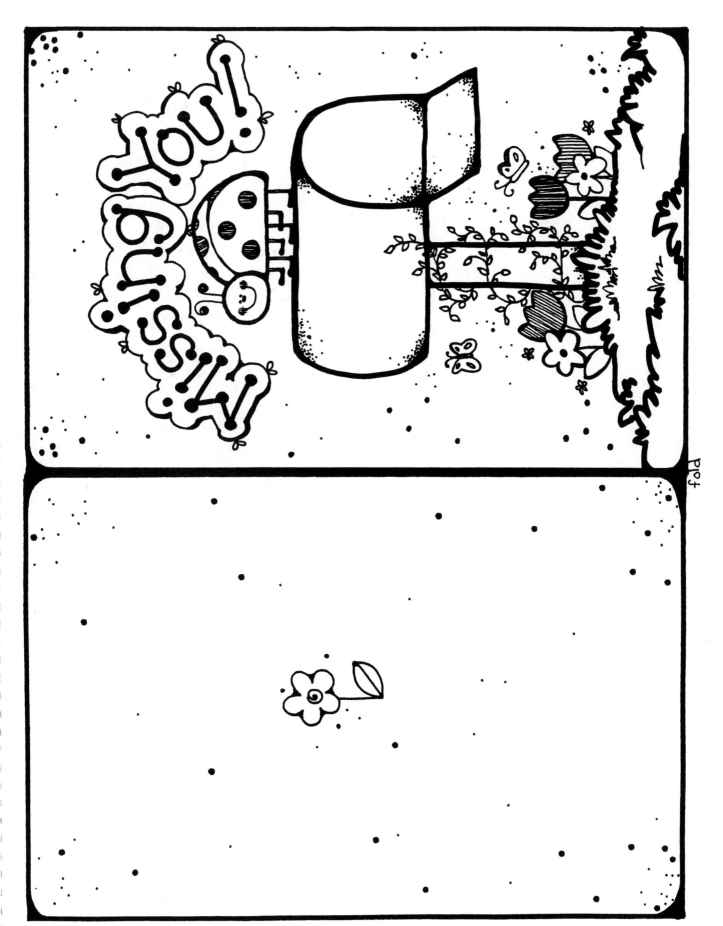

fold

285

way to GO!

This book belongs to...

name

class

grade

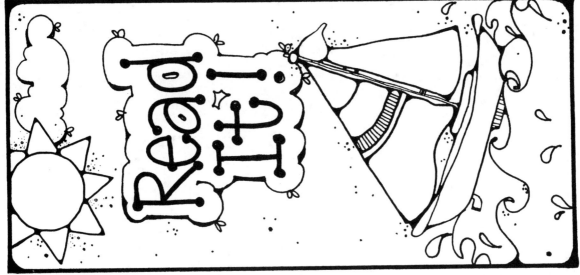

Read All About It!

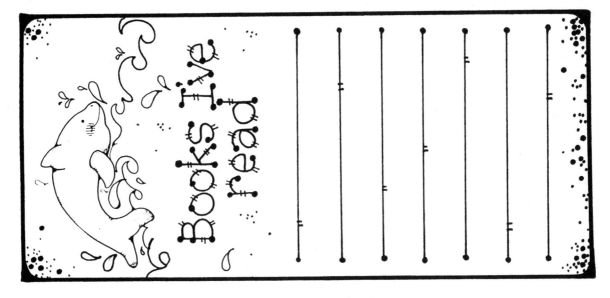

Books I've read

Funshine!

This book belongs to

Summer Reading

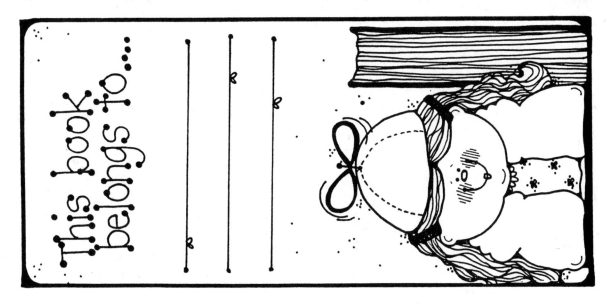

This book belongs to...

SCHOOL'S OUT !!

299

fold

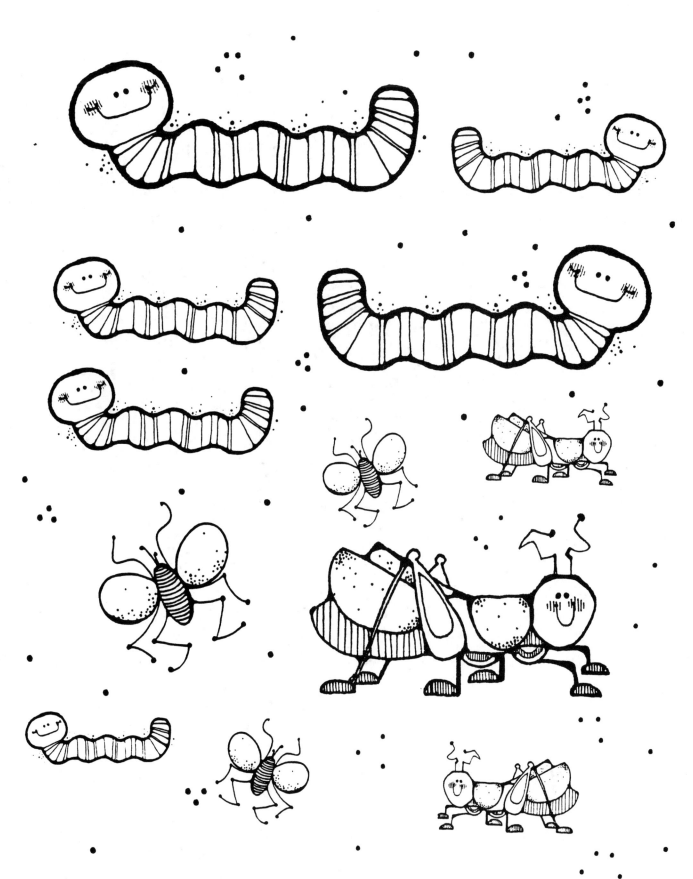

PEAS

CARROTS

RADISHES

311

Sunshine

fold

313

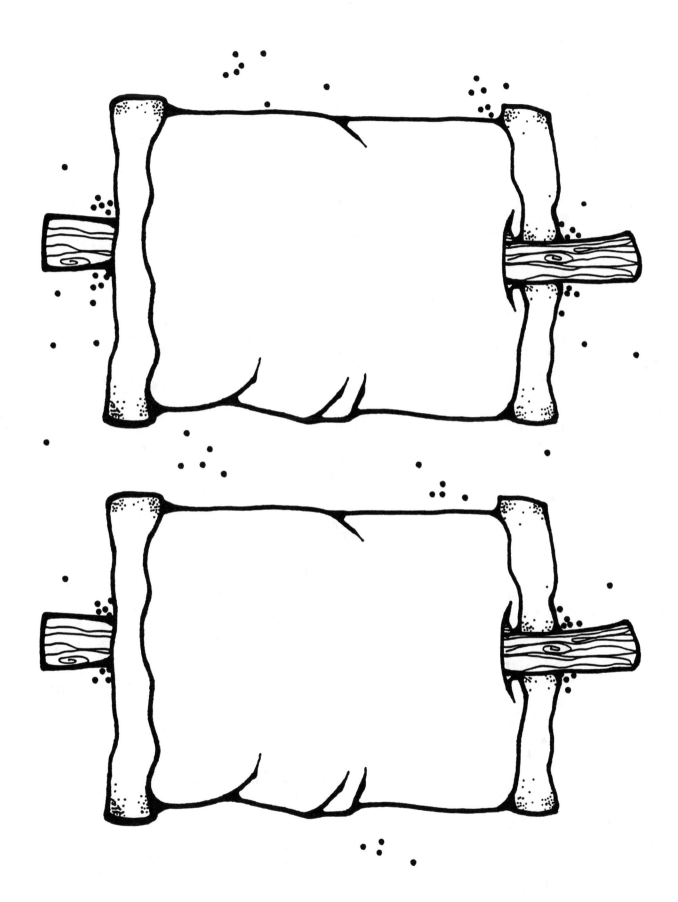

fold

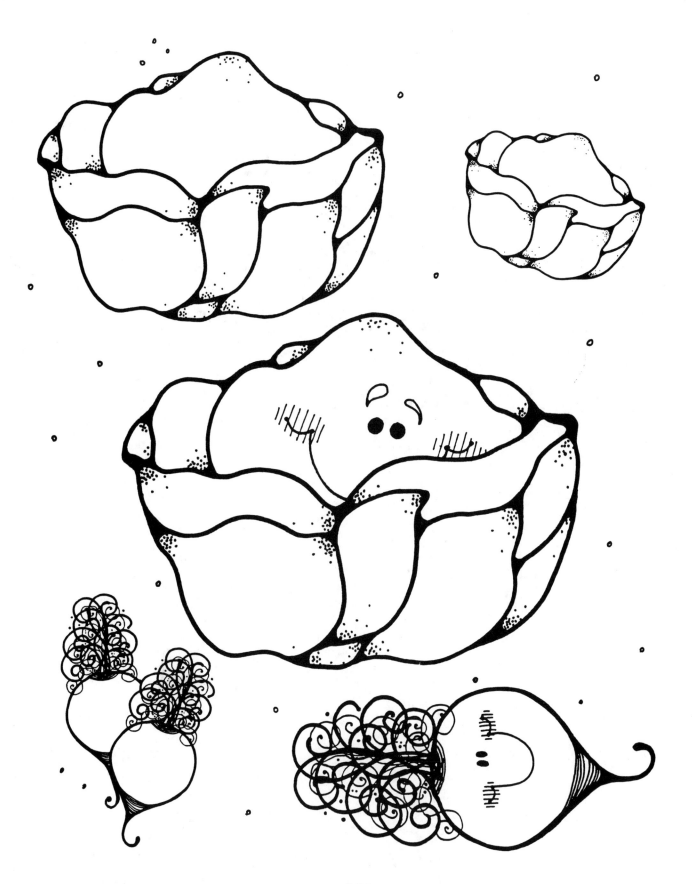

321

Nothing "BEETS" a great Volunteer !

GREAT WORK!

TRY OUTS...

SOCCER SCHEDULE

GOOD SPORT AWARD

_____
name

_____
date   teacher

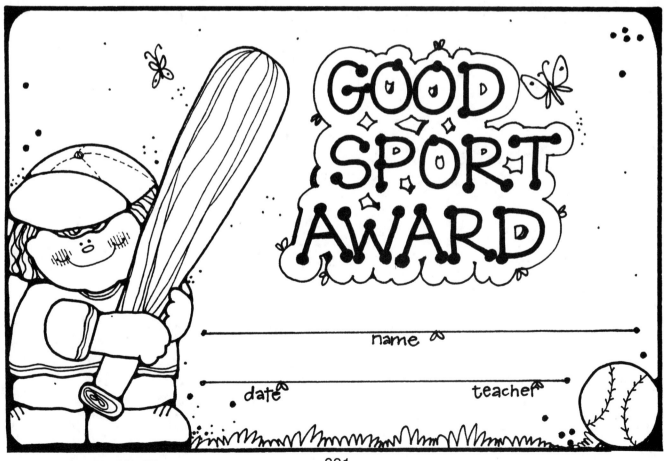

GOOD SPORT AWARD

_____
name

_____
date   teacher

Baseball

Baseball Schedule

Best Friends

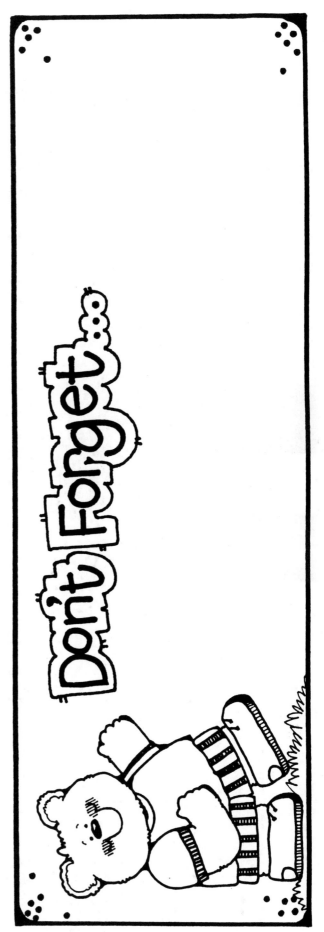

Don't Forget...

341

Reminder to my Dad...

Reminder to my Mom...

Graduation

Graduation

Certificate of Merit

Presented to

for

date

teacher

Graduation

this certifies that

_____

has successfully completed

_____

date _____ teacher

Graduation

this certifies that

_____

has successfully completed

_____

date _____ teacher

355

FUND RAISER

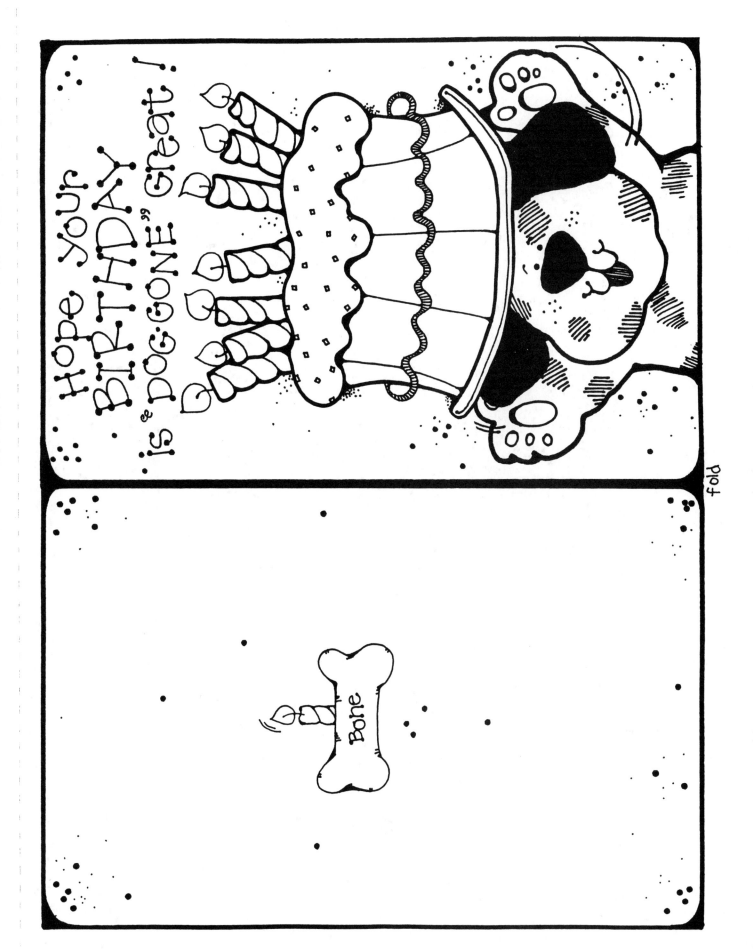

fold

363

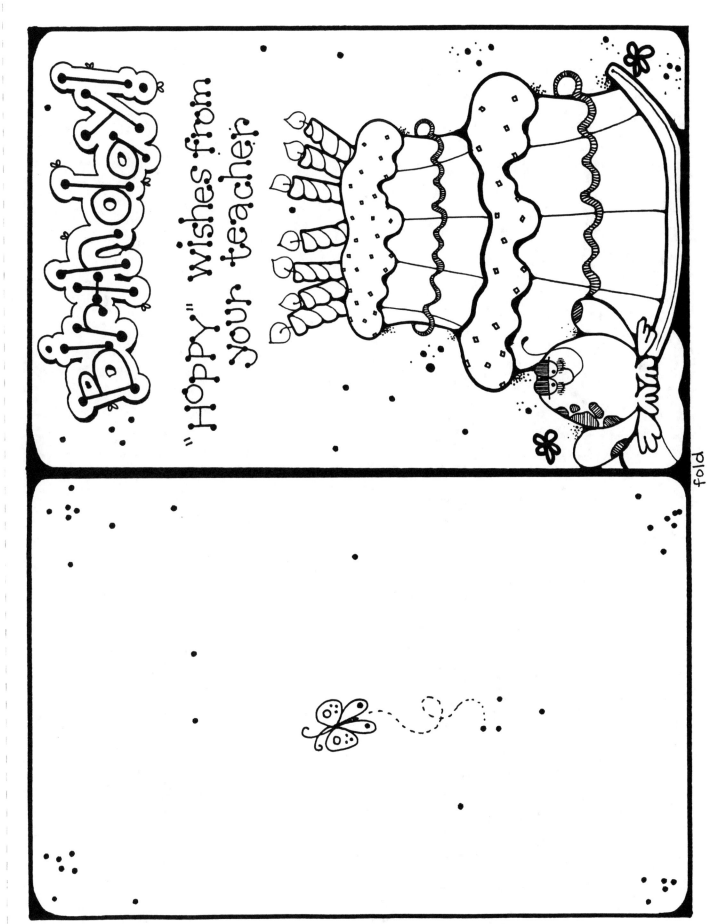

Birthday!

"Hoppy" wishes from
your teacher

fold

T.V Worth Watching...

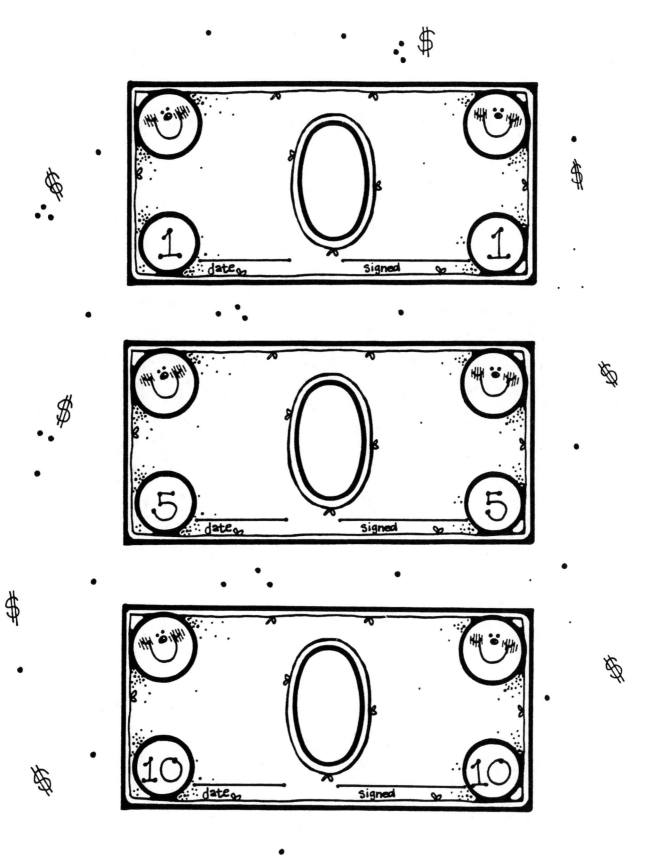

fold

377

You're DINOMITE!

"SEA" THE PROGRESS!

name

date